RHS

T0008932

Ultimate Sticker Book
TREES AND LEAVES

DK | Penguin Random House

With thanks to Ben Hoare for first edition text
on pages 6–7, 8–9, and 12–13

Senior Editor Kritika Gupta
Editor Abi Maxwell
US Senior Editor Shannon Beatty
Senior Art Editor Roohi Rais
Design Assistant Sif Nørskov
Illustrators Mohd Zishan, Rachael Hare
Deputy Managing Editor Roohi Sehgal
Managing Editors Monica Saigal, Penny Smith
Managing Art Editor Ivy Sengupta
DTP Designers Dheeraj Singh, Mohd Rizwan,
Syed Md Farhan
Picture Research Administrator Vagisha Pushp
Senior Jacket Designer Rashika Kachroo
Production Editor Becky Fallowfield
Senior Production Controller Ben Radley
Delhi Creative Head Malavika Talukder
Art Director Mabel Chan
Publisher Francesca Young
Managing Director Sarah Larter

Royal Horticultural Society
Consultant Helen Bostock
Editor Simon Maughan
Books Publishing Manager Helen Griffin
Head of Editorial Tom Howard

This American Edition, 2024
Previously published as
Ultimate Sticker Book: RHS Trees and Leaves (2006)
by DK Publishing,
a division of Penguin Random House LLC
1745 Broadway, 20th Floor, New York, NY 10019
in association with The Royal Horticultural Society

Copyright © 2006, 2024 Dorling Kindersley Limited
24 25 26 27 28 10 9 8 7 6 5 4 3 2 1
001–341095–May/2024

MIX
Paper | Supporting
responsible forestry
FSC™ C018179

This book was made with Forest
Stewardship Council™ certified
paper—one small step in DK's
commitment to a sustainable future.
Learn more at
www.dk.com/uk/information/
sustainability

Activities

Here are the six different types of activities
that you will find inside this book. Have fun!

Find it!

Hunt for the correct
stickers that fit
the blank spaces.

Follow!

Follow the trail
and put the correct
stickers on the pages.

Match it!

Match the correct
sticker with each picture
to complete the images.

Make it!

Put stickers on
the pages to create
your own scene.

Fit it!

Find the stickers that
fit the blank spaces and
complete the big picture.

Guess it!

Try the fun sticker
quiz. All the answers
are in the book!

Acknowledgments

The publisher would like to thank the following for their kind permission to reproduce their photographs:
(Key: a=above; b=below/bottom; c=center; f=far; l=left; r=right; t=top)

1 Alamy Stock Photo: Botany vision (cra). **Dreamstime.com:** Pascal Halder (tl). **Getty Images / iStock:** E+ / OGphoto (br). **Shutterstock.com:** Dina Rogatnykh (cla). **2–3 Alamy Stock Photo:** Blickwinkel / P. Frischknecht. **2–9 Dreamstime.com:** Aga7ta (texture). **4 Alamy Stock Photo:** Nigel Cattlin (tc). **Dreamstime.com:** Anna Kucherova (clb). **4–5 Dreamstime.com:** Worldfoto (bc). **6 Alamy Stock Photo:** Michiel Vaartjes (clb). **Dreamstime.com:** Gerald D. Tang (cra). **Shutterstock.com:** Olga S photography (crb). **7 Dreamstime.com:** Slowmotiongli (tl). **Getty Images / iStock:** Brittak (br); Urbancow (cla). **Getty Images:** Stone / Ed Reschke (cra). **8 Dreamstime.com:** Konstantinos A (cra); Russwitherington (cla); Pixelelfe (cb). **Getty Images / iStock:** Difydave (bc). **9 Alamy Stock Photo:** Botany vision (tr). **Dreamstime.com:** Tamara Kulikova (tl); Christopher Wood (cl). **Getty Images / iStock:** E+ / OGphoto (br). **Shutterstock.com:** Dina Rogatnykh (cr). **10–11 Alamy Stock Photo:** Nature Picture Library / Will Watson. **12–16 Dreamstime.com:** Aga7ta (texture). **12 Alamy Stock Photo:** Yuriy Brykaylo (clb); Panther Media Gmbh / Loflo69 (tl); John Eveson (tr). **13 Alamy Stock Photo:** Florapix (tr); Dia Karanouh (tl); Mint Photography / Stockimo (clb). **Getty Images / iStock:** E+ / Mammuth (crb). **14–15 Getty Images / iStock:** Orla. **16 Alamy Stock Photo:** Scott Camazine (tr). **Dreamstime.com:** Natalya Aleksahina (ca); Vladvitek (cra); Alexstar (cla); Anastasiia Malinich (cb); Hsagencia (br); Worldfoto (bl). **Getty Images / iStock:** Dgwildlife (crb); E+ / OGphoto (cr). **Shutterstock.com:** Dina Rogatnykh (tl). **18 123RF.com:** Micah Bowerbank (cb, bl/X2); Photographieundmehr (cr); Thatchakon Hinngoen (cb/heart leaf, fbl/X2). **Alamy Stock Photo:** Blickwinkel / P. Frischknecht (X4, br/X2); Dorling Kindersley ltd / Matthew Ward (crb/Cupressaceae). **Depositphotos Inc:** Scis65 (crb, fbr/X2). **Shutterstock.com:** Robybret (clb). **19 Alamy Stock Photo:** Scott Camazine (tr, br/X2); Nigel Cattlin (fclb/X2). **Dreamstime.com:** Fotofermer (cla, bl/X2); Valeriya Rychkova (cra, fbl/X2); Scruggelgreen (crb/X2); Jure Porenta (fcrb/X2); Worldfoto (clb/X2, fcrb/Tree X2); Anna Kucherova (fbr/X2). **Getty Images / iStock:** MahirAtes (tl); Robert Schneider (ca, crb/apple tree X2). **22 Alamy Stock Photo:** Michiel Vaartjes (cl). **Dreamstime.com:** Slowmotiongli (tr, br/X2); Gerald D. Tang (tl, fbr/X2). **Getty Images / iStock:** Brittak (crb); Urbancow (cra). **Getty Images:** Stone / Ed Reschke (cb, fbl/X2). **Shutterstock.com:** Olga S photography (ca, bl/X2). **23 Dreamstime.com:** Alexstar (tc, fbl/X2); Russwitherington (tl); Tamara Kulikova (tr, fbr/X2); Pixelelfe (c, bl/X2); Christopher Wood (cl); Anatolijs Gizenko (cra); Liligraphie (br/X2). **Getty Images / iStock:** Difydave (ca); E+ / OGphoto (cl). **Shutterstock.com:** Dina Rogatnykh (crb). **26 Alamy Stock Photo:** Blickwinkel / Mcphoto / Hrm (br). **Dreamstime.com:** Atoss1 (cb); Anna Kucherova (tr/X2, bc, fbr/X2); Jessamine (tc/X2); Maksym Bondarchuk (tl, tr, cl); Roman Samokhin (ca/X2); Yuliia Davydenko (cra/X2); Dusan Kostic (c); Lesuhova (cr/X2); Anton Ignatenco (cb/X2, bc/X2); Valentyn75 (clb/X2); Inna Kyselova (clb); Nemolovskaja (fbl/X2). **Shutterstock.com:** Potapov Alexander (bl). **27 Alamy Stock Photo:** Yuriy Brykaylo (cl); Panther Media Gmbh / Loflo69 (tl); John Eveson (tc, fclb/X2); Florapix (tr); Dia Karanouh (cra); Mint Photography / Stockimo (cr, crb/X2). **Dreamstime.com:** Tetiana Kovalenko (fbr/X2); Hana Richterova (fbl/X2); Alfio Scisetti (bl/X2); Anastasiia Malinich (br/X2). **Getty Images / iStock:** E+ / Mammuth (c, fcrb/X2). **30 Alamy Stock Photo:** Nature Picture Library / Andy Sands (tl). **Dreamstime.com:** Bobbrooky (cra, bl/X2); Zestmarina (tr, br/Earthworm X2); Slowmotiongli (cla); Isselee (br/X2); Gucio55 / Grzegorz Gust (fbr/X2). **Getty Images / iStock:** AZCat (cb, fbl/X2); Dgwildlife (tc); Michel Viard (ca). **31 123RF.com:** Photographieundmehr (fbl/Leaf X2). **Alamy Stock Photo:** Nature Picture Library / Andy Sands (bl/X2); Panther Media Gmbh / Loflo69 (fclb/X2); Michel Viard (clb/Culemborg X2). **Dreamstime.com:** Bobbrooky (fcrb/X2); Zestmarina (crb/Earthworm X2); Pascal Halder (fbl/X2); Anatolijs Gizenko (br/X2); Ronstik (fbr/X2); Hana Richterova (bl/holly Ilex X2); Tetiana Kovalenko (br/Juniperus X2); Liligraphie (fbr/Apple tree X2). **Getty Images / iStock:** Brittak (fcrb/ Golden chain X2); Michel Viard (clb/X2); E+ / OGphoto (crb/X2). **Shutterstock.com:** Dina Rogatnykh (fclb/Paulownia X2)

Cover images: *Front:* **123RF.com:** Thatchakon Hinngoen tc/ (bl); **Depositphotos Inc:** Scis65 crb, clb; **Dreamstime.com:** Natalya Aleksahina cra, Alexstar cl, Anatolijs Gizenko tl/ (flowers), Tamara Kulikova bl, Pranee Mankit tl, Nigel Spiers tl/ (Leaf), Christopher Wood tr, Zerbor bc; **Getty Images / iStock:** Dgwildlife bc/ (squirrel), Alexander Dunkel br, E+ / OGphoto ftr; **Shutterstock.com:** Robybret clb/ (branch); *Back:* **123RF.com:** Thatchakon Hinngoen tc/ (leaf), bl; **Depositphotos Inc:** Scis65 tr; **Dreamstime.com:** Natalya Aleksahina clb, Alexstar tl, Anatolijs Gizenko cr, Kuhar br, Tamara Kulikova tc, Pranee Mankit cra, Nigel Spiers crb; **Getty Images / iStock:** E+ / OGphoto ftl; **Shutterstock.com:** Robybret cl

All other images © Dorling Kindersley

Trees and leaves

Plants that have woody stems and grow very tall are called trees. Different parts of a tree such as branches, trunk, and leaves, all work together to help it grow. Trees can be found everywhere, from forests and parks, to backyards and streets.

The leaves produce food for the tree.

Pear tree

Pear trees have flat and glossy leaves, which are dark green in color. They can grow to be up to 49 ft (15 m) tall.

The bark has lots of tiny pores that allow oxygen to reach inside.

The trunk is connected to the roots underground.

Leaf shapes

Leaves can be of different shapes and sizes. Here are some common leaf shapes.

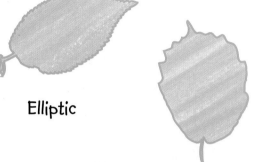

Elliptic

Round

Needlelike

Scalelike

Heart-shaped

Oblong

Branches grow out of the trunk. The smaller branches end in twigs, from which the leaves sprout.

Blooming flowers attract pollinators.

Sprouting

The seed will sprout, or germinate, in the presence of water, air, and at a suitable temperature. It swells and splits open, giving way to a small root.

Roots

The tiny root grows downward. It anchors the plant to the soil. A small, green shoot also grows upward through the soil.

Sapling

Gradually, these small shoots begin to grow upward. With enough sunlight and water, the first leaves of the plant unfurl and a new tree is born.

The seeds of an apple are found in a core in the middle of the fruit.

Seed

A tiny seed contains all the nutrients that a young plant needs to start growing. It has a tough coat for protection.

Follow!

From seed to tree

Trees grow out of tiny seeds. With time, these seeds grow into saplings and then big trees. It can take many years for a tree to reach its full height and some trees can grow to be thousands of years old. Follow the trail to see how a small apple seed turns into a big apple tree.

Young tree

While the tree is old enough to make its own food, it will take some more time to produce fruit.

5

Flowering

As spring comes, the trees bear flowers. The white-pink flowers contain nectar and pollen. These attract a host of insects that allow flowers to grow into fruit (also called pollination).

6

7

Fruiting

The spring blooms produce apples by the fall. An apple tree in good health can bear fruit for over 100 years.

Trees that lose their leaves

The leaves of some trees change color in the fall and then drop off. In the cold, dark winter months these trees stop growing, but in the spring, new green leaves appear. Trees that do this are called deciduous.

Quaking aspen

This tree can be identified by the rustling sound its leaves make in the breeze. It has rounded, heart-shaped leaves that turn gold in the fall.

Weeping willow

This tree is named for its long, trailing branches. It has narrow, oval leaves. Willows grow best in moist soil near ponds or lakes.

White oak

This big tree can grow up to 60–150 ft (18–45 m) high. It has jagged leaves with rounded edges. The tree produces acorns that mature in a single season and drop off in the fall.

Horse chestnut

This big tree sprouts clusters of tall, white flowers in spring. Its seeds are the nuts that are called "conkers." Its leaves turn from green to orange-red in the fall.

Silver birch

Lovely silver-white bark gives this tree its name. In spring it grows long, droopy, pale yellow flowers, which are called catkins.

Red maple

Maple trees are famous for their spectacular fall colors. Their hard, pale wood is used to make furniture.

The leaves of deciduous trees may turn red, orange, or yellow in the fall.

Laburnum

Lovely, bright yellow flowers cover this tree in late spring and summer. However, all of its parts are actually poisonous! Take care not to get too close.

Find it! Seeds, fruits, and flowers

Trees reproduce by making seeds. In many trees, the seeds form from flowers, and can be encased by fleshy fruit or hard nuts. Some fruits and seeds are spread by the wind or simply fall to the ground, while others are spread by the animals that eat them and poop them out.

Acorns

The nuts of oak trees are called acorns. An acorn is green at first, but turns brown as it ripens. Finally, it drops to the ground.

Conkers

A conker is the seed of the horse chestnut tree. The game of conkers has been played by children since the 19th century.

Elderberries

These dark, shiny berries grow on the elder tree in the fall. You can use them to make wine and jam.

Sycamore Keys

The sycamore's seeds are called keys. They are shaped like mini propellers. When they drop off the tree, they spin around and fly, traveling farther.

Plums

Usually planted for their fruit, plum trees are small in size. When young, the plums on the trees are green. They turn red-purple as they grow.

Magnolias

Magnolias were one of the first flower-bearing trees on Earth. The blooms of this ancient tree can be up to 10 in (25 cm) across. They can have a strong fragrance.

Foxglove trees

A popular choice for backyards and parks, this tree is also known as the princess tree. Its flowers are lilac on the outside and blotchy yellow on the inside.

Kowhais

The kowhais grow up to 33 ft (10 m) in height and have yellow flowers bunched together in small clusters. Their pods grow after flowering and each pod contains six or more seeds.

Flowering dogwoods

The flowering dogwoods are short, bushy trees. Their white and pink flowers make for a beautiful display.

Create your own orchard

Make it!

An orchard is an area dedicated to growing trees that produce fruit and nuts. Orchards can be big or small in size, sometimes with more than one variety of trees. Apple, plum, peach, and walnut are some of the trees that can be found in orchards. Fill up the scene with stickers of trees and fruit to create your own orchard.

Common holly

The spiny leaves of holly make it harder for animals, such as deer, to eat them. While the berries are important winter food for wildlife, they are not safe for humans to eat.

Douglas fir

This tree's natural habitat is the Rocky Mountains of North America. Squirrels and birds find the seeds in its cones irresistible.

Juniper

The juniper is a prickly bush that grows on mountains, rocky hillsides, and high plateaus. It thrives in unfavorable places where not many other trees can grow. Its dark berries can be used to flavor different foods and drinks.

Match it!

Trees that keep their leaves

Some trees have green leaves all year round, and so they are called evergreen. Their leaves are waxy and usually look like spiky needles or scales. Many evergreen trees produce tough cones, which are actually its fruit!

Cedar

When the wood of the cedar tree is cut, it has a wonderful spicy smell. Cedar trees originally come from North Africa and the Mediterranean.

Scots pine

At one time, these pines were part of mighty forests that covered much of Scotland. The forests declined as people cut down trees to make space for livestock. The climate also became wetter, making conditions less favorable for pine trees.

Yew

Yews live for many hundreds of years and they are a common sight in old churchyards. The older they get, the more twisted and crooked their trunks become.

Cypress

There are many different types of trees in the Cypress family. This elegant variety is popular in gardens.

Find it!

Tree homes

Trees are home to many different types of creatures. From the high branches to the deep roots, trees not only provide food, but they also provide shelter.

squirrel

Bat

Magpie

Tree bumblebee

14

Owl

Worm

Beetle

Tree life

Read about some of the animals, bugs, and birds that live in the different parts of a tree.
Reward yourself with a sticker for every animal home you learn about.

Magpie

Magpies make their nests in the branches. These birds build their home with a dome and a side entrance.

Squirrel

Squirrels build their nests, called dreys, hidden high up in the tree branches.

Tree bumblebee

These bumblebees live in tree cavities and use old bird nests to make their homes.

Owl

Owls need large cavities in the tree's trunk or bigger branches to nest in.

Bat

Bats prefer to rest in dark, hidden places, so hollow tree trunks make for an ideal home for them.

Beetle

Some female beetles prefer to lay their eggs under dead tree bark or fallen branches.

Worm

Worms can be found around the roots of a tree. They burrow into the earth and mix the soil, which helps trees to grow.

1. Blooming flowers attract pollinators. True or false?

2. What happens to a seed in the presence of water, air, and at a suitable temperature?

3. Name the tree that sprouts clusters of tall, white flowers in spring.

4. The leaves of which trees usually turn red, orange, or yellow in the fall?

5. What are the nuts of an oak tree called?

6. The flowering dogwoods are tall trees. True or false?

Guess it!

Sticker quiz

Reward yourself with a leaf sticker for each question you answer correctly.

7. Squirrels and birds love the seeds in the cones of which tree?

8. What are the nests made by squirrels called?

9. Which part of a tree is connected to the roots underground?

10. Which creepy-crawly can be found around the roots of a tree?

1.True 2. It sprouts, or germinates 3. Horse chestnut 4. Deciduous trees 5. Acorns 6. False 7. Douglas fir 8. Dreys 9. The trunk 10. Worm